# Venus, Jupiter

## William Doreski

Copyright© 2023 William Doreski
ISBN: 978-81-963161-7-4

First Edition: 2023
Rs. 200/-

Cyberwit.net
HIG 45 Kaushambi Kunj, Kalindipuram
Allahabad - 211011 (U.P.) India
http://www.cyberwit.net
Tel: +(91) 9415091004
E-mail: info@cyberwit.net

No part of this book may be reproduced or transmitted in any form or by any means, electronic, mechanical, photocopying, or otherwise, without the express written consent of William Doreski.

Printed at VCORE.

These poems have previously appeared in *Agave, Anobium, Anthem Journal, Arboreal Magazine, Behemoth Review, Big Windows Review, Black Mirror, Blue Five Notebook, Blue Hour, Bond Street Review, Breadcrumb Scabs, Bright Flash Literary Review, The Cabinet of Heed, Canto, Cardinal Points, Casserole, Chaotic Merge, Charleston Anvil, Cossack Review, Creepy Gnome, Cumberland River Review, Dark Forest, Dewpoint, East Coast Literary Review, Em Dash, Eskimo Pie, Feed, Florida English, Furious Gazelle, Gingerbread Ritual, Grus Grus, Hirschworth, Jellyfish Whispers, JMWW, Journal of Compressed Arts, Kaleidotrope, Lantern Magazine, Legends, Literary Mary, Loch Raven, Milo Review, The Mud Chronicles, New Guard, Pacifica, Planisphere Q, Poetry Porch, Poets for Living Waters, Random Sample, Red Lemon Review, Revue Post, Riddled with Arrows, Riverbabble, Scintilla, The Shore, Sketchbook, Sledgehammer Lit, Standards, Sunlit, SVJ Online, Symmetry Pebbles, Thin Air, Tomorrow and Tomorrow, Turtle Island Quarterly, Two Thirds North, Whisperings, Wilderness House,* and *Word Fountain.* Many thanks to the editors of these journals.

# In Memory of Andrew Glaze

How many words men have dragged downwards with themselves and made partakers more or less of their own fall. Having originally an honorable significance, they have yet, with the deterioration and degeneration of those that used them or those about whom they were used, deteriorated or degenerated too.

Walt Whitman, "Words" (*Daybooks and Notebooks* volume III)

# Contents

# From the Spirit Garden

Sprung from balls of matted rootlets,
parasitic and clammy white,
Indian-pipe so pleased Dickinson
that Mabel Todd painted it
to emboss on the cloth binding
of the poet's collected letters.

As you kneel to stroke the waxy stems
to see them blacken from handling
I recall that Mohicans derived
eye-lotion from part of this plant.
Was it from roots? Stem? The flower
that eventually crowns each column?

Much as I like this morbid growth
I fear that touching it might spread
the concept if not the fact
of decay. You laugh because
I keep my distance, cringing
as I watch. Nothing frightens you.

Nothing in nature disturbs you
the way your failing memory does,
or your lapses into the Polish
you can't remember learning
as a child. Every June this species
ratchets up beside the driveway,

this corpse-plant or ghost-flower
lacking chlorophyll and leaves;
and every spring we admire the way
it grows erect with fruiting
in honor of the rotted matter
on which all fresh effort feeds.

# A Runic Manuscript

My course in poetry and math
concludes with an equation
unsolvable because no one
knows what values to enter.
Truth? Beauty? The day after,
I drive down a shabby cul-de-sac.

Gray houses gloom in the chill.
Penned Dobermans bark and snarl.
Last night a garage burned down
and the firefighters reported
that a spirit rose with the smoke.
They found no scorched carcass, though,
only a charred runic manuscript.

I'd like to see it, but police
suspect it's sorcery and fear
someone might read it aloud,
so have locked it safely away.
They don't realize that it contains
the values required to solve
the equation I invented
to confound my students. The stink
of fire smuts the neighborhood.

The ruined garage lies so flat
in a sneer of cinders that no one
could determine from the rubble
what it had looked like in life.

The children of the neighborhood
have lined up to urinate one
by one on the debris. A local
custom, an old man informs me.

The brief November day fades
in a grimace of crimson sky.
As I drive away a whiff
of ammonia sickens me,
and I understand that the runes,
however magical, like
my obtuse homemade equation,
no longer function or apply.

# Orphic August Landscape

Spongy boletus mushrooms
gather around a pine stump
like mourners at a funeral pyre.

Although they're edible enough,
I'm not tempted to claim them—
their poise and attentive look

too poignant for me to disturb.
The brook rattling down from hills
the color of antique jewelry

expresses itself without shame.
Insects with terrible antennae
creep up and down the tree trunks.

The last landscape Orpheus saw
before descending into Hades
looked much like this one but

trimmed with belief in the gods.
If I could conjure up such faith
I could decipher the stony voice

of the brook and understand
why following it to its source
high on a slope with a distant

view of Boston would answer
questions I haven't learned to ask.
I would also know why mushrooms

ring the stump, why wispy threads
of their mycelium have burrowed
here and not in the richer soil

beside the brook. The mushrooms
are only the fruit of this effort.
But like Orpheus they linger

atop a gloomy underground
in which their great dreams fester.
If I believed, I'd learn why I should

or shouldn't enter this dark,
 the crackle of the running brook
a self-refreshing chorus.

# The Dreams Everyone Should Learn from Plants.

Along the sandy roadside
bunchberry flaunts four petals.
I walk here daily to encourage
my heart to interact with the world.
Every spring, wildflowers launch
their little sermons, dedicated
to keep the planet rolling.

But every year, fewer examples
of fewer species apply themselves
to the task of cheering the drab
places to which I'm committed.
No more trout lily, clintonia,
lady slipper, anemone, wild
ginger or trailing arbutus.

All thrived along this stretch
of town road until their roots
failed to go dormant in faded
winters that didn't freeze the soil.
I realize that I also have failed
to go dormant and dream the dreams
everyone should learn from plants.

Dreams of rich, mingled textures
and sparks the whole town can see.
Dreams of ripening decay.

Dreams of elongated fruiting
to assure the species continues.
Dreams of fauna and flora
blooming in lust and harmony.

When I return from my walk
I'll lie a moment on the sofa
and think underground thoughts.
But even if firmly sculpted
they may be too unseasonable
to let me nap comfortably
and dream as I know I should.

# We Must Consider Our Legacy

Maybe we'll leave a rusty stain
or two, a touch of dry rot.
Summer is like that: a tingle
of rain, followed by drought of flesh
and bone, the back roads heaving.
You expect me to clean the chimney,

service the gas heater, poison
caterpillars eating the hemlocks.
You want me to dust off the cats
and rouse them to cheer the storms
that warp and craze the landscape.
We must consider our legacy—

a clash of competing angles
and tremble of pale intrusions.
We must keep a detailed journal
of our daily quarrels, noting
dominant flavors and colors.
Crickets extemporize in the weeds.

Such music can't go unanswered,
but history suggests that it does.
Thousands of miles away, artillery
shivers whole civilizations.
We could be cringing in a cellar
with our parts neatly concealed.

We could be exploded in the street
with our parts scattered for scrap.
The stains and rot we leave behind
will speak for us with undertones
others will be too busy to hear.
Just as well. The next generation

will distribute its own disorder,
and moss will thicken over it.
Hard words will crack in the frost
and the cats will peer with wonder
as spirits trapped for centuries
flutter in the chill and disperse.

# Caretaker of Rooms I Dread

Absorbing the stammer of crows
doesn't render me crow-like
but alerts me to nouns like roadkill
and decay. August days whisper
of crickets and downloaded music
simpering through earbuds to addle
the adolescent minds I expect
to teach the glories of Keats and Yeats.
Yet in my recurring dream of rooms
sprawling haunted down grave corridors
I detect a musty nostalgia
not for the dead but for the living.

Caretaker of these rooms I dread,
I pause to fumble for a light switch,
but the light casts shadows that move.
The crows at dawn dare me to follow
these creased and greasy shadows,
but the people who cast them live
far away, unaware they're haunting
rooms I dream of sweeping, vacuuming,
dusting and mopping once a week.

Emily the senior editor
cresting the San Francisco hills,
Karl the retired historian
fishing sluggish prairie rivers,
Ken winding down a career
in an elementary school framed

by puckered Connecticut hills,
Charlotte closing her restaurant
in a rich Atlanta suburb
after decades of rave reviews.

I recognize their shadows and hope
that by switching on the light
I'm not disturbing their sleep.
The crows have made enough noise
so fly off with a few last clucks.
Some morning I'll fail to exit
those dream-rooms, and maybe then
my lost friends will feel a tremor
or at least a gust of cold air
and realize some creepy place
somewhere has shut forever.

# Stalked by the Otherworld

Late winter afternoon ghosts,
bits of wry incandescence,
flit tree to tree, following me.
I'm not afraid of such rags.
Harmless but curious, they drift

over fallen trees and skip across
the pleated brook, trailing sparks
of cold sunlight. In the open
at the fly pond they dissipate
with inaudible sighs, regretting

their fragile state of being.
I don't know if they're spirits
extracted from crumpled flesh
or created sui generis
with a chuckle of pure energy.

Since childhood I've been aware
that forested tracts foster them,
that they avoid large clearings
and never trespass in suburbs
too well-trimmed to conceal them.

The fly pond has frozen. The surface
looks too complex to support
my reckless weight, so I stand
on the shore and admire the flex
of elongated dusky colors.

Most of the snow has melted,
but patches retain the boot tracks
of someone who isn't me.
Can the ghosts distinguish us?
They watch from the red pine grove,

waiting to trail me back to the road.
If it gets too dark, I'll lose them
in the shadows, their tissues
too dainty to flaunt without gusts
of spectrum sieving through them.

I turn from the pond and imagine
excited whispers as the ghosts
regroup in puffs of ether.
Maybe the same winter ghosts
have been stalking me all my life.

I won't let these flimsy constructions
impose such a haunting on me.
The woods are too shaky to stand
in the gust of the terrible scream
these shabby creatures expect.

# Some Local Archeology

In the ruins of the high school
I find, among shards and cinders,
bits of human bone. They glow
like opals, intelligent even
in their fragmentary state.
You with your metal detector
scout for coins and other trash,
your grimace focused so firmly
I wouldn't dream of disturbing you.
I'm going to collect all the bone
to calculate the mass of life
lost when the old structure burned,
twenty years before I was born.
No one bothered to bulldoze the site.
No one cares that the town no longer
sends its adolescents to school.
For many years they've stayed home,
birthing from the age of thirteen,
shipping half their human crop
every year to state institutions.
The bone-bits are so weathered
they're almost wholly mineral,
fossilized scraps of people
we might have attempted to love,
or at least tolerate. Ivy,
that ironic vine, shrouds the walls
with their gaping window holes
framing views of violet hills.
The blocks of reddish sandstone

retain a certain integrity,
the material itself much older
than the ruins of Athens or Rome.
You find an Indian head penny
and a liberty dime. Let's quit
for now. You can buy us lunch,
and I'll show you the bones I've found
and maybe you can name them.

# Double Negative

A slew of scratched-out pages
litters the room where someone
deeply unpublished has died.
Police asked me to identify
the half-written, self-rejected
novel he left dismembered.
A cry of peacocks shatters
the limpid and ill-lit scene.
The cops shudder and turn away.
Maybe the hurricane plodding
through the Caribbean frightened
this writer to self-immolate
in all this indecent manuscript.
Maybe disbelievers facing
a distraught moon unlimbered
volleys of rhetoric to blotch
the climactic scene when man
and woman wrestle naked fates
in shivers of pulleys and gears.
The peacocks decorate the dark
because someone's authentic vision
planted them in the farmyard
of a broad-brimmed immigrant
from an unexplored geography.
The force of law doesn't apply
to the rings of Saturn, the space
between mutually corrupting stars,
so the pages can't be salvaged
although I can almost read through

the furious scrawl overlaid
by a badly weathered mind.
I wouldn't want my own laundry
hung on a stranger's clothesline
for the peacocks to satirize
and police to photograph
and then admit isn't evidence
of a double negative: the crime
of wrongly convicting oneself.

# This Imagined Paris

The boulevards pour over us
with plain geometric conviction.
Everyone is masked and humbled
by the simmering global virus.
Paris has never looked so raw,
the cafes nearly deserted,
half the museums zippered shut.
The rebuilding of Notre Dame
proceeds so slowly the workers
look Gothic yet post-historical.

We sip our lattes with caution,
keeping our voices pastoral
to avoid frightening others.
Odd that traffic hasn't abated.
Cars nose each other like dogs.
Produce trucks from Normandy
and the Loire Valley shoulder past
with arrogance predating the plague.

We have always lived this Paris
of dominate gray palette
on either side of the Atlantic—
the Luxembourg gardens
brisk with shadowy flirtations,
the Louvre with its great flowering,
Montmartre looming over us,
the Seine fed by every river
in Europe, Asia, America.

When we leave the café and walk
toward the spike of the Eiffel Tower,
which I've always feared to ascend,
we may find ourselves implanting
dinosaur tracks in the sidewalks
of Boston, the fish-stink harbor
brimming with its fleet of islands.
Or maybe we're on Manhattan,
that slab of construction presenting
the world's least healable wound.

But this time we're here in Paris.
The Jardin des Plantes at noon
ripples with a breeze the color
of authentic French, the women
masked so fashionably no one
can distinguish them from figures
of capable imagination
more forcefully sculpted than us.

# A Circle of Folding Chairs

A circle of folding chairs
stands in a cold but snowless
December meadow. Who or what
will convene? I choose a chair
and sit. Wind has flattened the grass,
the frostbitten stalks too stiff

to flex and resist. I realize,
after a while, that the chairs
aren't all vacant, that daylight ghosts
occupy several. I know them,
although their names have faded
and their faces eddy like smoke.

I'll sit awhile and try to recall
the good or bad times we shared,
but there's no use speaking
since the distance from one chair
to the next spans several decades.
I focus on a stretch of barbed wire

rusting along a fieldstone wall.
No cattle to contain, no sheep
for a cheerful border collie
to herd with quick little circles.
Not a house in sight, only a well
capped with a sheet of plywood

to keep children from falling in.
The ghosts aren't aware of me.
I'm too large and clumsy for their world,
even seated on cold metal.
Who placed these chairs here? Someone
borrowed them from a church vestry,

someone still among the living
who knew these ghosts would convene
this afternoon in this meadow.
Did I load them into my pickup
and drive them here this morning,
then return to see what has happened?

No, someone else, someone attuned
to the windy chords resounding
at year's end, someone who rhymes
the lilt of meadow with the dead
still among us, the gray light swirling
with a thousand voiceless regrets.

# The Magi Seem Authentic

Setting out feeders and scattering
cracked corn for turkeys, I sample
the cold like a new Beaujolais.
Sip, swill, spit out into the gray.
Chemical warfare in Syria,
a man pushed from a subway platform
to die a crescent-shaped death.

No wonder the oncoming rain
feels personal as an insult.
No wonder my cigar-shaped breath
clots into fog and falls in the grass.
If a white Christmas should arrive
it will mean a total erasure.
Still, the Magi seem authentic,

struggling across the outer fringe
of the Roman Empire to bring
their produce to honor a child.
If I could mount a camel
without laughing and losing balance
I'd join them to make a foursome.
As I turn to re-enter the house

the turkeys dash from the woods
to peck corn and roll in the dirt.
Yesterday two slept upside-down
in a bed of pine needles. Their feet

were pronged like tuning forks. The reek
of poison will drift from Syria
to spoil my day of reading books

about people I never met:
Baudelaire, Robert Duncan, Cato.
Their faces will form in the cold
metallic rain, then drift away
with postmortem sighs so palpable
they could be my own, remaindered
after a night of halfhearted love.

# My Father's Pea Soup

The pea soup my father brewed
years before his death remains
our primary source of nourishment.
Scoop a bowlful, heat it
over a wood fire. Microwave

won't touch it. The gas range
doesn't impress it. The view
from our fourth-floor apartment
doesn't even skim its surface.
We must tote it to the park

and break off rose bush and lilac
and stoke a fire under the pot.
The police take so long to arrive
that we've heated it and eaten
and returned to our love-nest

before the patrol car screeches
into the park and shudders.
You'd like to save up and buy
a bag of ordinary groceries,
but respect for my late father

requires us to finish his soup.
The bucket isn't bottomless,
but the soup expands with age,
renewing itself. Eat faster
in larger bowlfuls and maybe

someday we can deplete it.
If we don't, it will crawl
from the pail some grisly night
to smother and digest us.
Of course I'm only teasing.

It's ordinary pea soup, green
as your eyes and innocent
of all but vegetable desires,
its vitamin content unimpeached,
its vitality purely benign.

# In the Mournful Supermarket

In the mournful supermarket the meat looks stripped from auto wrecks, the milk has yellowed to sulfur, the baked goods could anchor yachts. I browse with an empty shopping cart while people around me, still panicked by the recent plague, snatch up canned beans and packages of dry pasta. I want to find something edible enough to sustain me through the threatening weather already pouting at the windows. I need rolls or buns and condiments spicy enough to disguise the taste of whatever dead creature I fry in my cast iron skillet. Rats scamper under the produce bins. Their tails dangle like earthworms on rainy sidewalks. They are the only fresh meat in sight. Behind the deli counter, the butcher snarls like a chainsaw. He wants to know why I'm disdaining his cold cuts. Pressed ham, roast beef, olive loaf, turkey, and chicken. Because they look like the plastic food you see in cheap restaurant windows. Because they ARE the plastic food you see in cheap restaurant windows. He doesn't deny it but wonders why I think plastic food isn't good enough for me.  I would rather buy one of those slabs of cannibal meat and cook it on the gas grill outside where the stink of death can dissipate. The butcher wraps a shapeless blob and flings it into my cart. I selected a package of stony rolls and head for the checkout line. Already some people have been waiting so long they've skeletonized. I wheel around their cobwebbed remains and out the door. No one calls after me, no one tries to stop me, the weather booming in the parking lot loud as an empire collapsing.

# Lounging in Your Lounge Pants

In your house at the edge of town
the kitchen sink sports three faucets:
town water, well water, hot water.
The town water tastes of chorine,
the well water reeks of iron,
the hot water squeals and emits
the spirit of the former owner.

You lounge about in lounge pants
while I pack my bag for my trip
to the dismal side of the moon.
We're too old for the raucous sex
this neighborhood likes to indulge.
We're too timid to nail each other
to crosses spiked in the churchyard
to discipline freethinkers like us.

I'm sorry to leave you lounging
in your lounge pants, but duty
calls me to my early vocation—
freelance astronaut, unpaid.
This house of awkward proportions
feels restless, about to rip itself
from its foundations and bolt.

I wish the water were drinkable,
but tasting either cold tap
puckers me like a rotten orange.
You'll be okay for a month or two

while I'm whirling among the stars.
I'll return with a valuable stash
of meteorites and rare metals—
enough to finance us for years.

You'll still be lounging in lounge pants
as if you hadn't entertained
a hundred lovers in my absence—
flushing them all down the drain.
with town or well water or maybe
scaring them to death by loosing
the hot water's misty ghost.

# Picking a Baby

Picking a baby from a litter isn't easy. Some speak only in runes, while others rev like unmuffled engines. Some vote Libertarian, while others adhere to the Stalinist line of thought. Some wear capes, others sport dancing tights, which don't go well with diapers. Some already use port-a-potties, while others are busy inventing a better flush toilet. Some eat with a spoon, while others try to harpoon the family pet. Some are boys or girls; others reject simple binaries. Some believe the impending parent must be a god, others believe that role belongs to carnivores. Some advocate for the underdog while others believe dog should eat dog. I lean over a crib full of these little darlings and reach in with asbestos gloves. They all look up, alert as amoebas. One tries to bite; one tries to set fire to the glove. That's the one I want, the budding arsonist. Look at how it clenches its little face, striking a spark in my heart.

# A Scenario I Expect to Sell to the Movies

The desk lamp you sent from Sweden
has fallen and smashed. The rubble
of its pottery base invokes

the Second World War, which ended
with my birth. To clean up the mess,
you lend me your latest boyfriend,

fresh from Moscow. He speaks no English,
but smiles as he wields a dustpan.
Meanwhile I'm trying to write

about the afterglow of romance,
which also invokes the Second
World War. Your grandfather died

when Germany washed over Poland.
His ghost lingers like ozone after
a lightning strike. Your boyfriend,

a gangster, shows me a pistol
made in China. Nickel-plated,
it looks almost as dangerous

as you in your professional mood.
Your State Street office festers
with clients buying mutual funds.

Their checkbooks swing like barn doors.
Their faces cringe in Florida tans.
Daybreak over Boston Harbor

smelts in cloud cover so thick
the brokers mistake it for profit.
Your boyfriend lies down on my daybed

and snores the most innocent snore.
When did you say you'd pick him up?
I heft his shiny pistol

and pretend I'm a gangster like him.
Gusts of decay drift from Europe
where the war will never forget

itself, and the harbor goes limp
in the dead of winter. Your clients
have to wait as you order me

a replacement desk lamp to light
manuscript pages intended
to flash your glory to the world.

# Dye Storm

Someone has salted the clouds
with chemical and vegetable dyes.
First, successive waves of red fall,
washing over the sultry hills
with ravages of wine-dark hue.

Safe indoors, I watch the mockery
of blood-feud taint the distance
like the future I won't attend.
No wind, but trees shake off
the tint of their own volition.

Next a downpour of yellow
brightens the marsh and deploys
ecstasies even frogs accept
with turgid but sincere croaking.
I want to rush outside and bathe

in this color, but will it wash?
Better watch from a distance
as the rain turns blue, deep
indigo, declaring itself
in roils of toxic surf. The singers

of the Seventies would sport
in this dismal tincture, baring
their inner organs for approval
and clearing their throats forever.
I'm no longer eager to exit

into the dye storm. The grass wilts,
the late perennials droop. But now
a green slush trembles from the gray
and renews the haze with strata
of organic flattery so ripe

I could almost be young again.
But when I step outside, the air
has cleared, the storm forgotten,
and the drabs of early autumn
nuzzle me, cuddling up to stay.

# Make Mine Vanilla

My double-amputee friend
orders pistachio with shots.
My childhood called those tiny buds
of chocolate "Jimmies," but the boy
scooping ice cream from cardboard tubs
understands so clearly that the veins
of his temples throb with empathy.

He's eager to go to war
but too shy to ask my friend
which theater dissected him.
He's too young to remember the green
and flimsy broadcasts from Nam,
the footage speckled with gore,
the voiceovers stern but quivering.

My friend walks with dogged aplomb.
He struts yet favors those legs
custom-made in Virginia
by "regular folks who care."
Awkward on my four good limbs,
I order plain vanilla and tip
the boy behind the counter
enough to embarrass us both.

# Carcass in the Closet

The carcass dangling in the closet
dates from an earlier age
when everyone read Baudelaire.

Gutted and soaked in brine, drying
to a neutral shade of leather,
it represents the moment when

art and science concurred.
You want me to discard it
after many years of toting it

house to house all over
New England. You claim decadence
has lost its cache, replaced

by ugly populist politics.
I had hoped to finance retirement
by selling this well-cured hide

to a museum of the grotesque.
But in the age of pandemic
most small museums have closed

forever, their collections looted
and sold on eBay for bitcoins.
You claim to recognize this corpse.

Yes, he was famous in his day,
and won an Oscar for his role
as Abraham tending his flock

on screens as wide as billboards.
No disrespect intended but
when I found him dead on my lawn

the profit motive engulfed me.
Alright, I'll forgo the money
and bury him in the back yard

and hope he doesn't get restless.
You notice how sweet he smells?
Death must have come so gently

that his organs hardly noticed.
And now his empty skin-sack
has toughened into the softest suede

so that someone elegant, like you,
could fashion him into a coat,
if you don't mind a little haunting.

# Our Local Geyser

Our local geyser erupts
daily at five past noon. Tourists
gather on the post office steps
to match that gush with their own.
The superheated rock below
gnashes and tries to vocalize,
but vapor foils it: has done so
for eons of soggy display.

We locals consider the tourists
unruly for admiring such rank
and steamy overflow. Yet day
after day we accept their pesos,
Euros, Swiss francs, tattered rubles,
and serve them lunch without menus.
Drafts of Shipyard ale or tumblers
of domestic red wine snuff
that spark of rebellion no one
can afford to simply ignore.

The geyser rips through a slot
in Putnam Park, where dogs walk
their owners and sun themselves
without recalling that daily
on the dot the geyser inflames
the otherwise innocent landscape.
At the first low grumble they tug
their leashes and, with masters

in tow, retreat. The geyser flays
the noon light. The steam could kill.

The hot plume rises two or three
hundred feet before subsiding
into a water-fountain trickle,
which certain local children drink
in hopes of growing Satanic horns
and otherwise getting in touch
with the glamor of underground.

# Starry Clots of Tar

An oil spill decades ago
sprinkled starry clots of tar
in the dust and weeds. The sheriff
plucks one and crushes it
with plump thumb and sausage finger.
Whatever he's thinking remains

fossilized in his domestic brain.
Abandoned after the accident,
the underground pipeline still sulks
with its freight of homeless demons.
I want to dig to the metal
and tap a message in Morse code,

maybe a passage from Dante's
morbid and sadistic epic.
But the sheriff warns that rust
has surely perforated the line,
which has collapsed here and there,
rutting the landscape. Somewhere

in the afternoon heat a couple
engages in naked exercise,
shedding phosphorescent sweat-beads
of guilt they've never really felt.
They own too much oil stock.
Their houses in London and Cannes,

Vail and Greenwich, smirk at fools

who work for wages. The sheriff
doesn't feel that pain. He likes to think
he could arrest the people who built
this stinking old pipeline if only
they crept into his jurisdiction

with their tongues dangling in the dirt.
I fondle a tar-clot and wish
someone with inhuman appetite
would teach us to ingest and thrive on
debris like this, leaving a trail
and daring enemies to follow.

# Venus, Jupiter

Planets stray across yellow dusk.
Venus, Jupiter. Their discs,
arranged to deceive us, look shy
as dimples. You note the lack
of cunning, the overbite. You claim
the inhabitants of Venus loom
large on their planet, while those
of Jupiter, smocked in toxic gas,
leer in marbled skins too tough
for our conventions to penetrate.

I'd say, "human conventions,"
but for you, great personifier,
every gesture counts. My drink
huddles on the table. Amber,
clarified and clarifying,
it withholds itself in flavors
only ripest adults can enjoy.

You disdain my taste and judgment.
You disdain my attempt to view
the roaming planets with ten
power binoculars, blinding me
to the sighs of garden and cluck
of woodpeckers at the suet.

Must I spend every moment on Earth?
Apparently so. A chill arises
from the addled topsoil I spent

the afternoon weeding. Autumn
will veil this landscape and shame me
into accepting its little truths.

You think Keats understood the frail
but persistent goddess trapped
in ordinary skin. I greet her
daily, but she always turns her back
to hide her rhinestone smile, her face
murky as Jupiter's yet shining
brighter than Venus would without
a lascivious smut of cloud.

# Another Homeric Moment

With elliptical pulse in the sky
seven AM announces
the pearly instep of a morning

flavored with blood in urine.
Not the most pleasant hue. The cat
responsible may be dying

of cancer: a message to nail
on a mud-brick wall in the desert
outside Jerusalem where minds

meet and linger over thousands
of years of war. Our leaders
won't lead us into the desert

but into plush conference rooms
where carafes of spring water
stand around like flamingos

and microphones cringe in the paws
of reporters working in six
or eight languages at once.

What hues does the ear pick up?
Is the desert at dawn wine-drab
like the cat's litter? Kneeling

and scooping away the stain
solves nothing. The armies poised
at the edge of every desert

in the world solve nothing but the itch
to trigger more ovoid pulses
than the sky can accommodate.

The seven AM fire horns finish
their winsome noise. The red splotch
isn't politics. The cat looks

indifferent to the clues it leaves,
but the cancer, if it's there,
expects to keep its promise.

# After a Day of Open Vowels

After a day of open vowels,
the town shuffles on all fours
to drink from the shallow river
and sample a chemical sweetness
inert to casual analysis.
Strolling among blank storefronts
I wonder for the hundredth time
how Heidegger fell for Hitler,
whose razor of a template
oversimplified the night sky,
reducing the stars to dimples,
compressing light years to moments
a man might fold in a wallet,
a woman might press to her heart.

The town looks even shabbier
than usual. Beer cans, donut bags,
and cigarette butts decorate
every lawn. No parade this
holiday weekend. No one believes
in Labor Day, the final Monday
of the season. Heidegger believed
more deeply than anyone should.
His pale head bobbled like a moon
in a lake, his hands shuddered
as he scrawled in flawless German
his theory of the peasant gaze.

Why distemper and numb that awe
with Nazi horror? No wonder
after all those open vowels
and the eloquence of the rain
I feel a rage to be human
again, to shed my intellect
in honor of eroded mountains
flexing across the horizon,
rivers flashing among boulders
as old as the earth itself—
while upstairs in wooden houses
in the earnest shame of daylight
bored couples make whatever
they imagine will pass as love.

# In a Brown Indifferent Season

A powerful fist of bobcat
forms at the edge of the driveway.
Focused on a chipmunk poking
seed from last autumn's litter,
the whole being of hunger
congeals in a throb of muscle.
Watching from a safe distance,
I hope the chipmunk gets away,
but I also hope the bobcat's
appetite sates itself somehow.

Raking decayed leaves from beds
of perennials that won't appear
for another month defuses
the angst I've nursed all winter.
So what if I've retired shameless
into poverty? So what if friends
scattered over the continent
deflate, one by one, into palest
shades of green and blue? Lately

I've outlived a couple of students
whose habits destroyed organs
they hadn't realized they needed
to lubricate their moving parts.
Three or four others deflated
in crashes fueled by favorite liquors
and framed by oncoming headlights
on the wrong side of the highway.

Astronomers recently found
seven new planets orbiting
a relatively nearby star. Maybe
bobcats have already evolved
in those livable environments.
And maybe a carnivorous
lack of diffidence will inspire
worlds rich enough to allow
chipmunks to escape unharmed.

# Dover to Calais

The packet boat from Dover
to Calais keyholes from the harbor
into the open channel. Waves
compete in shades of gray too subtle
for painters to trifle with. Eyes
cross as we stand at the rail and sing

national anthems of nations
we hope we never have to visit.
You look tragic as a movie queen.
Your script drops from your fingers
and mashes into the raving sea.
Everyone on this boat secretes

wounds as pale and crude as toothpaste.
Everyone has spied on this nation
or that through several careers.
This boat reserves itself for drunks
who slur French and English equally,
leaving spoor from Scotland to Nice.

We aren't drunk but have slurred ourselves,
flesh and spirit, so badly
the captain welcomed us with alarm.
Look back at the chalk cliffs sketched
on the sea-gray sky. Their fossils
represent our primal intellects.

We've progressed enough to distinguish
igneous from sedimentary
from metamorphic rock. You close
your eyes and risk mal de mere.
You don't want to see Calais approach
with pincer-like breakwaters

and wind-soured winter beach.
Too bad. We could swim back to Dover,
but the water's cold enough to wither
the most hirsute ambitions,
and the cliffs would clack like dentures
as we drowned a few yards from shore.

# The Steep Descent to the Lake

The steep descent to the lake
troubles me. How can I hustle
a bass boat down this slope,
or even a kayak or canoe?
The lake with stone-gray logic
lies flat. It's aware of itself
the way philosophers are aware

of Lake Geneva. But this lake
is too small to exclude itself
from the need to fish or paddle,
or swim, sink, and drown. Too shy
to cough up the many children
it has inhaled over a century
of summer camps. Too sullen

to confess that in a world of ideas
it has none. Neither do I,
but fishing for bass makes drama
as ripe as Voltaire, as cunning
as Kierkegaard roaming the streets
of Copenhagen, his tongue dangling
like a snotty old bandanna.

The gravel beach betrays nothing.
I peer into the water and spot
minnows dangling in clarity
I didn't detect from the heights.
Instead of fishing from a boat,

I could lie on the beach at the rim
of the lake and lap like a deer.

Maybe I'd inhale a minnow,
and maybe that would suffice
for a day of fishing. The slope,
when I climb it at day's end,
might ease itself out of pity,
allowing me to walk upright
as if I'd properly evolved.

# E Flat Major

In the concert hall the heat
of five hundred bodies dulls me.
As a string quartet saws Mozart
into many small pieces I doze.

A rain of paper rouses me.
Thousands of scrawled pages torn
from notebooks, lined paper,
shower from the space above the lights.

My grammar and high school essays,
resurrected to tickle the crowd.
Most people will mistake these pages
for discarded programs. They'll leave,

after applause, without reading
a word of my childhood scribbles.
Here's a scrap of my argument
for hanging old Silas Marner

and the author who stunted my growth.
And here's a leaf endorsing
the abolishing of school prayer
and the return of junior football.

My holograph resembles the fright
wig Andy Warhol sported
after a hard day faking art.
Only a few people even glance

at the paper sprinkling over them.
The rest shrug the mess to the floor
for the janitor to sweep up
and burn in the huge hot-air furnace

moaning below. I thought I tossed
this effluvia decades ago;
but this mangling of the Mozart
E flat major string quartet,

the third of the Hayden quartets,
precipitated paper from air
to impose, instead of grace notes,
the ignorance of my scrawl.

# The Vowels I Often Mistake for Your Name

The dark growls in primal shades
of gray and brown. Miles away,
you sleep as deeply as magma.
But above this corrupt small town
the stars wince and suffer, and cries
of owls linger much longer
than they should. Rising early

from a dream of being lost
between two small colleges,
the highways wrinkling like flesh,
I wonder how you'll survive
the years after I retire and die,
how you'll scrape my residue
off your favorite tall black shoes.

Today a dinner with guests
from the far side of the planet
will challenge me to interpret
my environment in startling terms.
How can I explain a landscape
of cringing villages and dour
glacial hills? How can I plot
the highways that separate as well
as conjoin our failing egos?

Mandarin speakers won't understand
unless I shape my speech to the will
of the T'ang poets everyone loves,

but I must include you despite
your absence because the cries
of the owls contained the vowels
I often mistake for your name.

Stars, owls, hills, and you sleeping
so profoundly the earth shakes—
and a landscape flakes away
like paint, revealing a structure
too simple for us to conceive.

# Road Maps

No one unfolds road maps
anymore. Delicious blue lines
of river, tiny black zippers
of railroad, and stocky red
of highways. Towns and cities

distinguished not only by type size
but by bullets of varied design.
Fragments of these maps appear,
sometimes, as smart phone apps;
but GPS has replaced them

in the collective imagination
to which Kerouac, Thoreau,
Darwin, and Rimbaud subscribed.
I can't read digital scrawls,
can't find your latest love-nest

with the navigation system
that tells my car where to drive.
Road maps, revised every year,
starred you in capital letters
with a bullet more like a bull's-eye,

but no one prints them anymore.
Maybe if I trace a river downstream
I'll arrive at the primal wetlands
where nightly you hold court.
But only a map that unfolds

in accordion pleats can expose
mysteries that fester in the dark.
No one else needs road maps
or geological survey maps
or thick old-fashioned atlases;

but how else can I trace you
through the analogical sublime
where the lines on the maps meet
and knot and gnarl and tangle,
and rivers mate with plain blue sea?

# Nothing but Haunting Can Satisfy

Sketching a naked torso
that could belong to either sex,
I'm clumsy as Picasso, eager
as Gauguin. Don't mistake it
for a self-portrait or botched
drawing of your own buff self.

This figure has haunted me
since childhood. It first appeared
when I dreamed the earth split open
and coughed up a pair of ghostly
white spectacles that later
hovered over the playground

and clapped an enormous thunder
that felled me in a heap of dross.
Later draped in black oilcloth
it climbed from that same ravine
and swaggered into the forest
with puckered blood-lips glowing.

Even in the daylight it roared
with the fervor of the village drunks
before one by one they died.
I saw it duck behind a bush
but leave its grimace seesawed
in the tender adolescent air.

I wipe my actual glasses to see
all the better how I've caught
the human taint that conceals it
from the nobler part of the mind.
You accuse me of obsession,
of fantastic cravings nothing

but haunting can satisfy. The sheet
of drawing paper crumples itself,
dissatisfied. I'll drive to town
and get the Sunday *Times* to prove
how calmly I can face the world,
regardless of what inhabits it.

# Soul Sale

When I ask Satan to sell my soul back to me, he says, "You can have it. What do I want with that filthy rag?" We're sitting in a coffee shop in Midtown. Buses hustle past, snoring and shaking the plate glass windows. "You have to accept payment," I say. "Contract law requires both parties to benefit from a transaction." The waitress refills our cups. She thinks Satan is cute, with his pert little mustache and his crimson cassock. She glares at me, a grumpy wrinkled old man, and sneers. She'd spill coffee into my lap if she weren't afraid of losing her job. "No benefit involved. You must realize that it's worthless," Satan explains. "If I accepted payment for returning it, I'd be adding to my burden of sin." "But if it's worthless, what does that say about me?" "You sold your soul. You sold it so long ago that it became obsolete. I made a poor investment. That's on me. Just take your soul and drink your coffee while it's hot." He hands me a slip of rumpled tissue. I tuck it into my shirt pocket. It's so tiny I'll probably lose it. "You might as well face it. Hell isn't for you. You wouldn't last five minutes before vaporizing." "What about Heaven?" I ask. "Yeah, sure," Satan says. "You wouldn't last a second."

# Weed Feed

Goldenrod, tansy, ragweed,
sorrel, plantain, and crabgrass.
The first hard frost flattens them.
Their roots withdraw to contemplate,

and their upper mass browns and decays.
I browse through the rusty trash
and trace the little humped tunnels
of mice going no place special.

Looking this closely at the world,
I find everything textured enough
to eat. But chewing on a stem
of ragweed's uninspiring,

the papery tasteless fiber
probably too nutritious
for my tired old corpse to absorb.
I flop on my back and look up

through breezy treetops where the light
crackles like a smashed windshield.
If only I could rise like bread
and become more fully myself—

if only the arrogance of weeds
flustered in my heart I'd name
myself Lord of the Flowers and crush
the ordinary public with scowls

toothed like the leaves of goldenrod.
But lying in the wilted clearing
in the creak and sway of pines, I hear
a better language rejecting me,

rejecting my entire species.
I can eat all the weeds I want,
but I won't learn how creepily
they renew, how forceful the seed.

# That Gioconda Moment

The crowd of tourists facing
the Mona Lisa congeals
into a gray singularity.

I've never trusted that painting,
or Pater's glib description,
which Yeats rewrote into verse.

The smile looks slightly manic,
the potato face seems rooted
in clammy earthen desires.

You expect me to worship
with those who look upon art
as the savior of their passions.

You want me to snap a selfie
with that fatuous smile askew
with a thousand old platitudes.

Look at the landscape looming
teary with mist behind her.
The trees look pubic, the streams

flowing through mythic places
one would rather read about
than visit while still in one's skin.

That landscape is the part of her
Leonardo declined to paint,
even to amuse her husband.

You know about such body parts,
and have cherished your own despite
the patina age has imposed.

The painting simmers with lust
that the lanky hairdo defies.
The wrinkled clothing is the shell

of the subject's private self,
which you dare me to reveal
by blowing the portrait a kiss.

# Florida Mystery Object

Either washed up on the beach
by yesterday's arrogant storm
or exposed by erosion, this
structure suggests the rib cage
of a creature extinct for eons.
Step inside. The play of light
across these wooden slats casts
runes of indelible meaning.
We could co-author a treatise
on this prehistoric construction.

The smooth of Daytona Beach
seems to flow forever. The blue
of the Atlantic looks Homeric.
The wreckage of whatever this was
is drying gray into driftwood.
We must settle on a legend
before beachcombers wrench it
piece by piece from the sand.
We must transcribe the epic before
subject quarrels fatally with verb.

The day perfects itself as only
a luscious Florida day can.
Half-fossilized, the toothy slats loom.
The runes burn archaic phrases
into the sand. We can't read them,
but the sea lathering and stropping
its fore edge will soon erase them.

So we'd better start taking notes
even if they read like scripture
that confirms our lives of sin.

# Antique Bluebeards

All night as wind gnashes pine
I dream that antique bluebeards
overtake women I failed
to learn to love. Shallow water
splashes underfoot, Venice

sinking into the sea. Old friends
try to help. Their faces deflate
in primary colors. Their bodies
lilt in eerie Venetian dusk
and flutter inland to roost

on the grounds of Palladio
mansions left grinning with pride.
I swim with strokes as clumsy
as my penmanship. I swim out
to the cemetery isle to see

the grave of Ezra Pound.
I find it open, escaped.
He's the template for those bluebeards—
his cantos precede them all:
free verse abandoned in favor

of Fascist doggerel goosestep.
Soaking wet from my long swim
I dodge into the palace and hide
among the Doges. They accept me
as a political refuge

from the Romantic mode. The sea
brims over and over, smirking.
I can't bear sleeping any longer
so I shrug off the thick old men
draped over the women I failed.

With a clack I align my bones
and lurch to the bathroom like
Philip Larkin and listen hard,
hoping the wind won't name me
in conspiracies I can't support.

# Composed yet Decomposed

At the Point the fog horns bellow
in shades of gray so desperate
I can feel the rock shore tremble
with pity. The upthrust of schist
and pale weathered gneiss challenges
my shaky old legs, but I step
from ledge to ledge by faking
grace I've never received. Farewell
to the island view, the sailboats
that might be tacking out there.
Farewell to ghostly kayakers
slipping too close to the breaking surf.
The fog renders distance useless,
folds the shore and surf together.
One misstep and I'll break something
and flop like seafood while the gulls
peck out my liver and share it.
At low points, tide pools whisper
about crabs and barnacles and weed.
I try not to listen, but musings
in low tones the ear can't define
always distract me. By noon
this fluff will whisk itself away,
leaving a sheen on dimensions
too delicate or stubborn to hide,
but for now the imposture's complete.
No wonder I'm a little dizzy:
I forgot my dawn medication,
that creepy little pill that sears

the throat and settles like ballast.
In this density I'd forget
my name if it didn't adhere
in five syllables to my pulse.
Three terns pose against the gloom.
I'd snap a prize-winning photo
if the effort wouldn't topple me
into the foam. Better sit down
on a dry slab and recover
what remains of my senses.
I'll convince myself a horizon
still lurks out there to help me
distinguish upright from prone.

# The Bus for Malcontents

The bus for malcontents creeps
to the curb. The doors hiss open.
Should we board? The driver
stares straight ahead. No fare required.

We climb two steps and scan for seats.
It's crowded. Only one spot,
beside a crabbed old woman
clutching a paper sack of laundry.

I'll stand. With a diesel snort
the bus lurches toward the harbor
where we can re-baptize ourselves
to flense our petty little sins

or drown as gently as we please.
Our fellow passengers don't speak
or meet each other's eyes. The edge
of everything, drawn by sad artists,

flickers past, trailing a shadow.
Blocky buildings gnash like molars.
The bus-motion grips us, bone-breaking
handshake all over. I'd talk

off the spell, but my voice is a clot
of disconnected tissue, my mouth
is my grave. The long rubber mat
between the rows of seats writhes

with malignant intent. Windows
fog as spirits leave our bodies.
At last the bus stops, the doors
flap open, the driver slumps dead

at the wheel. We crowd off and scatter,
distancing from each other's mood.
The harbor gleams like fresh money,
ready to invest.  I catch you

before you throw your glance too far
to sea, the aqua horizon warped.
The bus leans sideways on two flat tires.
It will surely never run again.

A tow truck arrives to claim it,
but we can't recover from that ride,
the stink of its engine fouling us
with pigments too drab to erase.

# Self-Shedding, Ending with a Preposition

Human dust, our own shed cells,
powders us daily forever,
distinguished grime of the world.

How did we become so fragile,
so prone to quiet dissolution?
Does the dust ever become us

again, resuming basic functions?
Or is it debris, spoor, clue
to our most clueless moments?

At dusk the town lights struggle
to illuminate the darkest folds.
Traffic sputters home to house

and child, furniture sulking
after another day of dust.
Someone tries to read a book

as thick as a thigh. Someone pours
a drink the color of starlight.
We crumple into each other

with expressions milked almost dry.
The dust never settles. Lamplight
catches particles breezing

through heated indoor dimensions,
feeling for a surface to smut.
We shed ourselves completely

several times per lifetime. Snow
and rain aren't so persistent.
Should we be more respectful

of ourselves, and gather our dust
in plastic bags, add water,
and try to clone our modest egos?

Let's not bother. The lamplight
isn't entirely honest,
and the town, winking and blinking,

 will sneeze and snuffle human dust
until we've shed our skins and bared
everything the night sky lusts for.

# The Necessary Café

In the Necessary Café,
men brood and slouch in their seats
but women brighten like novas.
You, for instance, enlarge, enflame,

and shed twenty years of grief.
That red dress you abandoned
when your marriage to the count failed
returns to envelop and flatter

your girlish little figure.
Diamonds sprout all over you
and a pearly aura emanates
from the subatomic mesh

of your pores. I, however, sink
into myself like a boulder
in a marsh. The mud-taste thickens
my tongue, and the old waiter

with his stained apron resembles
a butcher hired to dismember
everything male about me.
Still, I remember my manners

and tip him for bring a last
round of cappuccinos, his smile
like a White Russian's in exile
between the wars. They're long dead,

though, Paris and Berlin too brisk
to tolerate such learned *angst*
in shadowy backstreets. We laugh
because you're so vibrant and I'm

so brittle and stale. We'll revert
to our late-life neutrality
when we leave this fetid café.
But let's enjoy our contrasts

for another hour or two,
the promise of your bold young ego,
the flash of diamonds, the drama
of my existential sneer,

the crowd plotting around us
like a hundred unwritten novels
bitter with grit of self-exile,
spiced with unrequited sex.

# Among the Insipid Hellos

Learning to use the telephone
means listening to dead folks chat
in those tinny voices you hate.

When you drive past cell towers
note the mist that always hovers
near the top. That's a fog of ghost

that haunts even conversations
between healthy youngish people
who don't believe the dust-smells

cling to them, don't realize spiders
have already eaten their organs.
You of immaculate male friends,

of summer dresses shaped like tulips,
of peaches ripening early
and peonies lasting till autumn,

have never heard the faintest buzz
of static on the airways. Yet there
among the insipid hellos

certain agate blossoms deploy
and force us to reconsider
the mauve light we cast when shadows

aren't enough. You talk all day,
text all night, and your phone glows
with a thousand fatal sunsets;

yet you believe your body contains
the capacity to chant the names
of a thousand failed deities.

No, you have to acknowledge
that the ghosts on the line are human,
and need you to anchor themselves

before they drown in the air.
Don't expect your hefty male friends
to intercede. They've noticed
already that the ghosts feel drawn
to you, stanzas of residue
clinging to nothing but the glow

you emit when you speak without
anyone watching: a wine breath
purple enough to sink ships.

# The Impulse to Fly

On the trail by the waterfall, I meet two people even older than me. They're hiking with canes instead of staffs. The man is ninety, the woman eight-nine. I can hear them appraise me, although their lips don't move. A little too young to be hiking alone, but probably divorced, unsociable, or just plain loner. The latter, I note. We discuss the state of things: the rich people in the village and their unholy greed; the small-time politicians fluffed with arrogance; the children who clump in parking lots to sneer. The schools remain closed because of pandemic and post-election anguish. Parents who work long hours can't home-school, and the kids won't hang around for classes on Zoom. We agree that the planet is clenching a fist. We agree that the waterfall in its lucid purity rebukes humanity. With a wave and farewell they set forth, caning their way back toward the car park, a couple of miles through the flimsy autumn forest. I follow at a safe distance. After half a mile, the woman sprouts wings and flits up through the trees and into the solid blue. After another quarter mile, the man does the same. I clutch their abandoned canes like a bundle of fasces. Maybe I'll reach my parked car before the impulse to fly overtakes me. Maybe not.

# Lime Shadows and Blue Rain

A day of stale geometries.
Clouds buckle and disperse.
Big thunderstorms nod and smile
en route to the Atlantic.

The universal solvent of sky
has rendered me gray with mildew.
Yet I retain a bus-station urge
to chat up strangers in the name

of battered mountainsides and brooks
that runneth over. Downtown
with grim clarity I decide
to orate to the trash can set

before the diner, the mailbox
smirking while its riveted seams rust.
When I'm proficient I'll nail
actual people with bombast

that will sever their otic nerves
and keep them sleepless for weeks.
No one has ever claimed or disclaimed
in the hues I'll emit. Rainbows

will dissipate in shame. Minerals
plotting deep in the crust will shed
their long-term prismatic ambitions.
I can't ask anyone to submit

their personal beauties to a cause
so pear-shaped it warps one's aura.
But certain fringed eyes turn my way,
and certain indelible notions

buck the prevailing west wind.
The day creeps on all fours and cries
like a kitten. It can't fool me.
Its tragic output betrays it

with lime shadows and blue rain;
and its consequent musings explain
the dolor of the post office
and the pain I like to nourish.

# Sifting the Ruins

Sifting the ruins for clues,
I find a metal file box
of letters I sent you many years
before we met. Some in English,

some in French, German, Chinese.
The dry old pages tremble like silk.
The words look raw as their source
in that lost Indo-European

ur-language, the one you speak
to lovers as you impale them
on their bluff, old-fashioned lust.
The light fails. Distant streetlamps

cast a brassy but useless glow.
I run a hand over a typescript
and read *heron, bygone, fop*.
What had I told you about life

in the marshes? I'll study
these letters when dawn sobers me
and I've showered away the stink
of this house you burned to the ground

to conceal forensic evidence
of your lack of human empathy.
A police car noses past. No one
can see me creeping in the shadows,

but I don't want to be shot
for looting so I lie so flat
my expression dims with ash.
That's how you remember me,

isn't it? Not our long August sail
across the Black Sea to Turkey
and back, but my weeping in church
as the old superstitions failed me.


My ashen face reminded you
of war before you were born,
so you swept me into the distance
where I've lingered ever since.

The patrol car moves on. The stink
clings and conforms to me
as I rise and clutch the letters
and feel them crumble and mingle.

Their languages are like minerals
combing under massive pressure
to form new chemical entities
I'm unqualified to assay.

# Dinosaur Pants

Put on these pants, run your hands
down your thighs. Like the scales?
Wearing dinosaur pants honors
the common pool of DNA
from which all poetics derive.
You wonder what dinosaurs left
inscribed or impressed in mud
besides their notorious pawprints.
Sometimes prowling riverbeds
in search of polished garden stones
I find in the sandstone ledge
runic scrawls a reptile claw
might have penned in a moment
of reflection on the forthcoming
and predictable mass extinction.
Although I can't read these marks
by touching them I feel a throb
in my brain that corresponds
to the ache for mutual expression
that binds us to trees and mice.
You know that feeling: a whisk
of fibers across tingling nerves,
a pleasure rooted too deeply
to betray its source. Wearing
dinosaur pants in public
proclaims your allegiance to facts
that foil the religious fools
who rely too much on one brave book
to shield them from the distance

that pours like milk through us all.
You look good in that tight fabric,
the green-gray scales flattering
your gunpowder complexion,
and your confident stride folding
and unfolding dinosaur-thoughts
that never go out of fashion.

# Life List

You ask if I keep a life list
for blue heron, great auk,
forty or fifty shades of warbler,
robin, bluebird, vireo, dodo.

Why should I check off birds as though
their flutters and cheeps responded
to some indecent proposal
made on my behalf by forces

derived from the earth's magnetic field?
You refer to a field guide
and binoculars. I possess
these appliances, but indulge them

only when the moment ripens
as some aerial confection
alights at the seed feeder
I've hung from a tall ash sapling

twenty feet from my back porch.
You can travel to the Hebrides
or Costa Rica or High Island,
Isles of Scilly or the Faroes.

You can hunker in hand-knit sweaters
at the rim of gray-green marsh
and peer at the quaking image
of a spoonbill in your spotting scope.

You can take notes on rare species
until cramp and chill numb your fingers.
I'm staying home to count
and arrange my books by color.

Slurping tea from a vulgar mug
and browsing in art books as thick
as my liver will ease me
to the very end of my life list,

where only three or four names appear,
none of them yours or mine
or anyone else hogging
dimensions we might want to share.

# August Blue Moon

At five AM the blue moon glows
like a hole through which the daylight
of a different world is bleeding.
Up to catch this phenomenon,
I've wrenched a muscle in my back
and bumped my head on a cabinet
so hard I gained an excess of stars
to accompany my glimpse of moon.

The atmosphere possesses a rare
quantity of blue, a chemical
layer dense enough to lave a bruise
on the cosmic mask the ether dons
whenever homo sapiens looks
beyond the immediate landscape.
Meanwhile with your soft hands folded
and the cats heaped on the bed

you snooze that disinterested snooze
I associate with minerals
buried deep in the planet's crust.
The natural world excludes the books
we've read to shape us to ourselves.
It also excludes the fear of death
that would preclude more expansion
of a crass if buoyant universe.

Yet I'm up to see a rare blue moon,
and you in sleep have fossilized

in the subtlest hues of agate.
Something insidious in the glare
of this watercolor satellite
alerts me to a weasel primping
at the edge of the deck I built
ten summers ago. The creature

preens like a cat; but because
it lacks shoulders its motions lack grace.
With a start it senses me, darts
away, leaving a comet's tail
flickering. Those are sparks of moon,
a sympathetic light that falls
on everything alive, a pageant
of malleable air. I peer as hard

as I can at the moon to memorize
its peculiar blue, then retreat indoors
to shower and shave as if days
like this brim as normally
as neap and ebb tides do—
the oceans of our interiors
slopping around those organs
too focused for moons to endorse.

# The Serial Killer's Van

This battered van could house us
if needed. I bought it cheap
from a serial killer's estate.

He roped his victims to tie-downs
and let them cringe awhile before
he performed his favorite rites

of love and religion. Speech acts
linger, so please don't listen.
No actual ghosts, only echoes.

The cream paint gives away
its former use, so let's paint it
puce, charcoal, parsley, or lipstick.

Then truck the old sofa to the dump.
Feel how smooth the transmission is,
how the engine's burble soothes one

into accepting whatever fate
offers in its offhand way.
A filthy old van, even with blood

scrubbed away and messages scratched
in the paint effaced out of pity.
But we'll renew every surface

before we move in with bunk beds

bolted to one wall and a bookshelf
and small desk opposite. Later

you'll be glad enough to live here
when the hurricanes hit and trees
crush ordinary houses. We'll park

in the hospital parking lot, safe
from contingency; and voices
of those half-forgotten victims

will chatter around us for comfort
as the wind beyond threatens
to lift every flimsy veil.

# An Act of Justice

You drove the car up the brush pile
and left it with headlights on
and engine off. You rolled the metal
roof from the house and sold it
to dishonest contractors cheating
our neighbor who raises Pekinese.
You rerouted water from the well
to flood the street and ice over
and trigger a dozen collisions.
You invested your retirement fund
in shipbreakers on the furthest shore
of the Indian Ocean. You sold
your dog to a Chinese restaurant,
which enslaved him as a bus boy.
Finally, you tipped the bed and spilled me
into a heap of dirty laundry
and tried to stuff me in the washer
where I'd go round and round forever.
I escaped and dashed outdoors and called
on the heavens for help. The weak
amber headlights pinned me against
a starless and ignoble sky.
The neighbor who raises Pekinese
phoned the police, who responded
with sighs of boredom. Their car
towed yours off the brush pile.
They arrested the contractors
and called Public Works to sand
the slippery road. They rescued

your dog from the restaurant where
he'd made a hundred dollars in tips.
They couldn't recover your funds
from the ship breakers, but maybe
that was a sound investment. Lastly,
they arrested me for knowing you,
an act of justice so abject
the stars broke through cloud cover
and wept a trillion ions of joy.

# Acknowledging Our Cybernetic Successors

Hooks and eyes, screws and zippers,
duct tape and staples. No need
for expensive surgery, extended
hospital care. Unzip, unhook,
pop out the bad organ, pop in
the new one. Rezip, re-hook,
smooth over the seam with duct tape.

No blood, bile, or lymph to spill,
the sealed systems warranted
for life, and even a life beyond.
No doubt this new human functions
better than we did in our prime.
Note the pointed forefingers
designed to work tiny keyboards.

Note the flap-ears styled for ear buds.
Note the LCD monitor: pulse,
temperature, sexual preference
on a scale of one to one hundred.
We could have ourselves rebuilt
to mate with the new generation,
but would have to mortgage ourselves

to Chinese speculators to pay
what our HMOs don't cover.
So we'll stay with the messy old
flesh-model, but maybe replace
with vinyl, copper, and rare earth

metals those parts that fail us
under great emotional pressure.

We'll never fully digitize,
like the dinosaurs, but survive
ourselves in the simplest terms—
leaving a smear, a residue
for our cybernetic successors
to sniff as they trundle across
a tundra of smoking ruin.

# A Coyote's Forepaw

The clarity of brief December
afternoon hikes to the beaver pond
flashes like glass in the sun.
Today, for example, I press
footprints into a crust of new snow,

crossing and partly erasing
tracks of deer, fox, coyote, skunk.
The woods, often logged over, look
scrawny as a cry of starvation.
No one I know has starved to death,

but every winter someone old
dies penniless and too proud to ask
the despised state government for help.
The cold numbing down from Canada
exhausts oil and wood supplies

and leaves nothing for the taxes
every town exacts in quantity.
Meanwhile the low December sun
peers through a bramble of saplings
and casts shadows so deep the tracks

open like craters of the moon.
No hunter, I rarely bother
to read the ground too closely,
but today I kneel to trace
with bare fingers the outline

of a coyote's forepaw and feel
the hunger vibrate in its bones.
Lank gray carcass of a beast:
I pity the shark-like appetite,
the ill temper that could drive it

to attack chained dogs and risk
a fatal mauling.  This coyote's
alone—no tracks of a nearby mate.
Even indoors, heated, books piled high
at my elbow, I couldn't face

the early dark the way this creature
does, howling down bare starlight
with one forepaw raised, a faint
trace of my human odor
clinging to the tips of the claws.

# The Owl Knows More About Blood

July heat tatters in pines.
Up at midnight reading Melville,
I hear a great horned owl tune up
to frighten mice and voles working
for grub. The hoot repeats, tolling

like a horror movie soundtrack.
For a moment, I'm small enough
to fill the craw of some creature
flexing through the night sky.
I remember my childhood dream

of white and bodiless spectacles
hovering over the playground.
Its appetite, a great unknown,
licked my heart and savored it.
I woke screaming so quietly

my fox terrier didn't stir.
Luminous in the graveyard shift,
the book flutters in my hands.
If I weren't holding tightly
it would flop away and hide

under the bed where everything
metamorphoses to monsters
that never completely grow up.
I'm reading "Benito Cereno,"
marveling at the shaving passage,

the razor slipped under the chin,
the nick, the tiny blood-splotch.
The owl knows more about blood
than Melville or me, but still
the depicted moment triumphs.

I grip the book so firmly
that the rags of heat fluttering
in the blackout become flesh,
torn and suffering but stubborn
in its duty to survive.

# A Cover Story for Grandma

Chatting outside the wash house,
we devise a cover story
for your granny, former KGB.
The mountains creak in the cold.
The wash house plumbing shudders.
Why should your granny's career,
terminated decades ago,
keep her out of the USA?
She'd enjoy the bleat of taxis
on Fifth Avenue, the yawn
of Bryce Canyon, lactation
of snowfall in the Rockies.
She'd shake hands with Republicans
and sample crab cakes and oysters
and taste a dozen Gallo wines
without blushing. But officially
she's excluded because the scars
of her victims glow in the dark
and her accent's rough with potholes
so deep they expose fossil bones.
But an alias will resolve her,
and the Russian government, eager
to expel her, will issue papers,
including a visa and green card
so gently forged they'll flatter
even the keenest official eye.
The cold today stands around
with both hands in its pockets.
We should drain the wash house plumbing

and close the camp for winter,
but I love the frown of mountains
as weather obsesses the summits,
don't you? Let's prepare our friends
to confront your granny's arrogance.
We'll claim she's really a Tsarist,
and like these eroded old mountains
has maintained her stance forever,
even if her fault lines show.

# Living in Moscow

Because we don't speak Russian,
the streets look too wide to cross
and the apartment blocks appear
forbidding as burial mounds.
Our two-room apartment loves us,
of course, with that tentative love
we associate with money.
And the women at the tea shop
speak in fuzzy gray English
in our presence so we can share
fragments of the massive gossip
that like a nuclear reaction
empowers their fuzzy gray lives.

In the expensive leather shop
a block off Red Square you wish
for a reindeer-hide briefcase.
But when I attempt to buy it
the clerk informs me that only
the stuffiest bureaucrats possess
this smut-colored accessory.
He wants a bribe, so I explain
that your lifelong blonde condition
descends from the royal family
of Argentina, and slip him
a sheaf of counterfeit Euros.
He brightens from every pore,
and I buy the briefcase with dollars
good enough to eat. Maybe later

he'll discover the Euros are fake,
but a fake bribe's good as a real one.

Strutting home with gleaming briefcase
you look like a candidate
for the Politburo. The long pink
summer day declines with regrets.
As we crouch in our tiny rooms
traffic snores down frightening streets,
shaking the city as if something
huge were having boisterous sex.

# On a Nabokov Short Story

Lacking a sheet of paper
to feed my manual typewriter,
I must step outside and scratch
my epic with a stick in snow
on the mountain behind your house.

Eventually it covers a slope
large enough for an Olympic
ski event. You're impressed but
preoccupied writing an essay
on a Nabokov short story
I've forgotten or never read.

The day whispers to itself, ruffling
hemlock fringe. Mice crackle beneath
snow cover, knuckling through tunnels.
My epic concerns the naissance
of our republic, barrels of rum
and beer, duels and adulteries.

Perhaps the Founding Fathers smoked
homemade cigars as thick as axe
handles. Perhaps those cigars
mixed pokeweed and marijuana
in the tobacco and stunned them
into writing a constitution
too eccentric for courts to parse.

You chuckle over your essay,
your prose burning with phrases
from Bakhtin. Your critical moves
dazzle like figure skating. But
when this essay appears in print
surly academics will scorn it
because you're not at Harvard.

The hillside gleams and my epic
solves entire worlds. But new snow
already fills my cursive scrawls,
so I step inside to shake off
the cold and read your essay,
product of an evolution
the rest of us haven't begun.

# Tomato Farm

At the tomato farm, long shivers
of irrigation ditch draw the eye
to vanishing-point perspective.

The bushes gloat tall and fungus-free
in ranks at least a mile long.
I envy the tomato brothers'

work ethic and savory results.
Would you like to tour the farm?
Note the footbridges linking rows

and the plank walkways to prevent
footfall from compacting soil.
Here's a tool shed painted black

so it won't reflect glare and scorch
nearby plants. A pump house also
in matte black hulks where a ditch

cuts perpendicular to feed
the long parallels. You note,
while stifling a little scream,

the occasional human hand
or foot thrust from the water.
No crime scene here, only slack

human carcasses donated
last winter when the shelters closed
for lack of funding. Police

collected the dead from the streets,
and the tomato brothers offered
to bury them free of charge.

Look how big and rich the tomatoes
have grown only eighty days
after planting. You needn't worry.

They'll taste as good as they look,
and even with your overbite
you're unlikely to draw blood.

# On the Mental Health of Seafood

Daffodils, grape hyacinth, violets
pepper a cleared space. The forest
envies these cultivars the way
seafood envies the vegetables
in the local market. You mean
nothing special to the heavy men
who peddle lobsters from the backs
of trucks on Friday afternoons—
merely another customer
hesitant, as most people are,
to drop a life form into a pot
of boiling water. But I like
the way you unpeg the claws
to allow them to open and grope
for the flesh of the oppressor
before you cook them forever
and wash down their tender meat
with gulps of Belvedere vodka.
And I like the way you ritualize
the cleanup by arranging the shells
in the fossil shape of the creature
before you formally consign
the scraps to the trash. The days
blossom so bravely in fact
and fiction. This First of May
you've celebrated with lobster,
vodka, and a bold new lover
chosen from available stock.
I like the way you rename them

after ancients. This one is Phidras,
but I don't recognize the source
in Greek myth or literature.
No matter. My flowers tremble
in the gusty dawn and reclaim me
from envy of men you select
for a moment of star-shaped pleasure
fresh from the bottom of the sea.

# The Problem of Anatomy

In the breeches-brown spring forest,
a woman walking a brown dog
avoids me, her face rambling off
to the northeast. Most hikers
and dog walkers halt in their tracks
to chat up strangers grubbing along.

But this woman suits herself—
perhaps afraid of landforms
padded with glacial accidentals
shaped like me. So the earth needs
purging. That's why seasons change.
No need to blame me for failed

caulking jobs, rivers splitting
on old seams, the slack of doctrines
over-preached all winter. The cries
of unknown birds insult the glare
of midday, into which that woman
propels her dog, which also

disdained to notice me peering
into a moss-framed clutch of flowers—
golden thread and anemone.
Maybe my concentration appalled
whatever she reserves for herself.
Maybe the horn in the center

of my forehead, the one I've yet

to grow, whispered to her. Always
the problem of anatomy.
Always the dark layer writhing
in the anger of the sun. Maybe
I could precipitate an eclipse

of the intellect. Maybe she fears
the ordinary part of me,
the function all women despise.
Maybe she'd rather not learn
how little faith I've retained
in my capacity to surprise.

# Science as the Letter S

The lab stinks of roasted meat.
The rat experiment has failed,
the college has yanked the funding.
Outdoors after months cringing
before a snarl of large wire cages,
I breathe freely and confess
to the withering sun that hubris
doomed my thesis and slaughtered
more rats than the pied piper could.

Curing viral effusions by high
voltage, frying relevant organs,
tickling and contorting the brain
works on paper but not on rats—
their bodies too understated
and their egos too undeveloped
to appreciate pure science
in its raw disinterested form.

The river lies bloated and wan
in its primordial trough. Odd
that I never noticed how sensual
its ripples, how brassy the light
stumbling over its requiems.
Insoluble vapors hiss and sob
like overeager sonneteers.
A kingfisher plumbs for trout.

I should revamp the lab in vague
but compelling pastels to scorch
the resident virus with beauty.
I could fill retorts and flasks
with red and green ink to express
theorems best left unexplored.
The resultant décor would wow
the dean into sexual ecstasies
compatible with fiscal relief.

Isn't that what French decadence
inspires? A thousand dead rats,
a million adrift in the Seine—
a river like this one but deep enough
to flatter barges from Belgium
and Germany. I wish I'd failed
my science courses, but peering
into the Bunsen burner I greeted
the genie of the flame and named him
after myself, and the slaughter
of expensive white rats followed.

Now the life of design has faded,
the crisp lab coats stained and limp
and sweating on their hangers.
The river limps along nonetheless,
and the meat smell gradually abates
as whatever was doctrinaire
or digital in the radiance
goes yellow and sanguine with age.

# Queen of the Island

The lake sports three hundred islands.
Searching requires weeks or months
of coast guard boats dropping clusters
of uniformed people toting food,
stretchers, radios, and blankets.
You could be anywhere. Eloping
with the ghost of your first husband,
leaving a note proclaiming yourself
Queen of the Island, sparked this search.

I expect to find you neither
dead nor alive. The winter islands
offer cottages ripe with canned goods
and easily burgled. You and the ghost
should find shelter and food enough
to keep your mutual body going,
but the star-spangled sex crime
of your dreams will never occur.

The cold lake laps gravel beaches.
When it freezes over, the search
will continue with snowmobiles
and even dogsleds. Roaring, barking,
the mob will scour every island
to find and punish you for tracing
yourself backward into vacuums
where the spirit disgorges itself
in fits of primary colors.

The lake shivers in its skin.
Under weak winter sun the water
looks black enough to swallow
the flaccid bulk of the cosmos.
Let's hope it doesn't come to that—
your crazy expression glowering
in a dark cottage, your ghost lover
trying to calm you as the creak
of the planet's axis amplifies
the very flaws you detected
two or three lifetimes ago.

# The Paddock

At the paddock where the mountain view dominates, I pause to snap a photo. You're trying to hurry me along. Snow has already started falling, and we're on foot two miles from home. Above the mountains, the clouds resemble the breath of massive creatures plowing through the sky. You don't see that? Then look at the groomed surface of the paddock. No hooves have disturbed this manicured ground since the leaves fell and the caretaker raked them away. See how dark this fine gravel is. Aren't you afraid of falling through it, down to the bedrock plotting below? You say you've never much liked horses. You claim to prefer animals small enough to cuddle in your lap. Maybe that's why you've gotten bored with me and want to hurry home. Go ahead. If I weren't afraid of the caretaker, whose moustache bristles like a pine, I'd erect my orange nylon tent in the middle of the paddock and spend a night absorbing the massive distance. The next day I'd return to you in a righteous state, and you'd have to accept whatever I told you about the stars, the mountains, the bedrock pulsing with lust. You'd have to believe me because when the ghost horses came after midnight and trampled me I somehow survived.

# Red-Inked Runes

Before dawn, I find you rigid
at the kitchen table, your face
a ceramic mask. Papers smut
the oak surface. Illegible
runic handwriting proves nothing,
as the police will later admit.
You're not actually here because
you returned to Ireland years ago,
leaving a faint trill of speech
in the streets of Jamaica Plain
where every shopkeeper knew you.

I hadn't spoken your name
for a decade, yet here you sit
with expressionless expression
and a cat crying at your feet.
Can you explain the runes scrawled
page after page in red ink?
You've spoiled my best fountain pen,
a Waterman, by clogging its point
with ink the police will describe
as blood. Your long hair has grayed
like a shadow. Your posture insists
on boarding-school poise you kept
until an accident bent your spine.
I touch your shoulder and you crumble
or fade, leaving me a handful
of irreducible yellow salts.

Certain a crime has committed
itself, I call the police
to consider the evidence.
When they arrive in a fluster
of blue lights, radios, and gun belts
of black patent leather they shake
their bullet heads and persuade me
nothing can be done. The day ends
as it began, naked and mewling,
with a sheaf of red-inked runes
and a handful of chemical dust
to scatter over my garden
in the faceless autumn dusk.

# As Vanishing Point Perspective Vanishes

Already the heat exfoliates
in layers of reprocessed wool.

Today I must face the fact
of slowly going blind. My doctor

will shrug that shrug learned long ago
as an intern on the night shift

when most of the horrors occur.
I should have stuck to science

in my undergraduate moment
when clarities leapt from the muddle

and offered to resolve the world.
I could have self-diagnosed

with established facts to lean on,
the pages of refereed journals

fluttering with flirtatious glee.
Armed with a medical license,

I could have accurately placed myself
in the post-Darwinian scheme.

You don't accept my darkening view,
my insistence that my vision

no longer explains anything,
no longer distinguishes toxic

from edible mushrooms, no longer
resolves the lines of force

represented by tall white pines.
The eye people will gather

around me and chant in Latin,
high priests half-demented

by their congregation's lack of faith.
You warn me not to be silly.

You claim that Doctor X understands
how vital my vanishing point

perspective is, how desperately
I process every text I meet.

But when I enter that den
of illegible eye charts, the man

himself will declare me hopeless
and scrawl a useless prescription

in holograph so illegible
it will mock me into the dark.

# Sad Weather Shopping

Dribbles on the supermarket floor.
I scrabble on the wet spot and fall.
Unhurt, I rise, but a woman
also falls, smacking her head,

which pops open. Cans of peas,
soup, pears in syrup, jars of mustard,
mayonnaise, peanut butter, and one
exotic bottle of soy sauce

tumble from the crack in her skull.
She rises, unsteady. I help her
to the service desk. Did she steal
that stuff or merely imagine it

into existence—her shopping list
materialized? The manager
can't charge her with shoplifting,
can't prove the contents of her head

came from his shelves. He offers
aspirin and a towel to wrap
her fractured tête for her doctor
to examine later. I tote

my groceries, neatly bagged,
to my car. Drizzly winter rain
soils the view of grizzled mountains.
The asphalt glooms like a frozen lake,

shallow with a bleak mud bottom.
If I were a fish I could swim all winter
despite my torpor. Bottom-feeder,
I'd prosper. Groceries loaded,

I drive away wondering how,
when her husband asks how
her day of dull errands has gone,
that woman will explain the crack


in her skull and the free groceries.
Probably she'll heal overnight.
Tomorrow she'll imagine a new
and longer shopping list, complete

with frozen turkey, loaves of bread,
and half gallon of milk crowding
against her medulla oblongata
to keep her completely sane.

# Fire Fox

Along the highway between Dublin
and Marlborough, the fire fox
races in a stream of blue sparks.

Driving alone after night class,
I glimpse this legend speeding
at the edge of the forest, trailing
a comet-tail so bright I blink
almost with pain.

The fire fox
rarely shows itself, a creature
of mossy ravines where hunters
die of heart attacks and decay
to skeletons before they're found.

*Vulpes ignis*, no specimen
ever examined by naturalists,
lives on a diet of starlight
and the melt of the earliest snows.

It speaks only to shamans
of certain long-extinct tribes
and doesn't bark or yowl or whimper
or otherwise betray emotion.

I've driven this road at night
for twenty years without catching

a hint of fire fox, yet here it is,
blazing just ahead.

I hit the brakes
not for fear of hitting it
but because I'm almost blind
with its glory.

The creature turns,
runs toward my stopped car and leaps
on the hood, pressing its face
to the windshield.

A perfect fox face,
pointed and elegant cone-nose,
liquid green eyes reflecting
and absorbing my stark expression.

It bares a thousand pointed teeth,
impossibly tiny quartz-like teeth
set with perfect little garnets
and grinning with good fellowship,

but realizes I'm hardly
the antique shaman required
to parse its riddles and spread
its semi-carnivorous word.

In a blast of blue startle,
it explodes to the heavy black line
of forest and douses itself
in the dark.

I drive away slowly,
the highway shaking with palsy
and the intellect drained from me—

the blue light of the fire fox
still burning far behind my eyes
where I'll never stop seeing it
or feeling its cosmic desire.

# The Book of Mountains

Swaggering over granite ledge,
The trail parallels high tension lines.
Tiring too quickly to savor
Tiny red-capped spikes of lichen
And moss-patches of purest felt,
I slacken and conform to the view.
Wachusett, Monadnock, Temple—
The bluff peaks ripple horizons
Pale with haze. Villages hunker
In the folds. A church steeple here
And there, a few pastures shaven
Into the dusty forest scruff.

A woman abrupt as the landscape
Primes herself in Manhattan
For a slot in big-time publishing
With a massive conglomerate
Of impeccable corporate ego
Flattered by her trim gray suits.
In childhood her Baptist father
Beat her silly with both testaments,
Teaching the power of the Word
Over the ravings of the body.
So I've written *The Book of Mountains*
To reclaim her for the present tense
With lyrics that prove that the Word
Solves the flesh as well as the spirit.

Let her sight along Fifth Avenue
And she'll detect me in the distance
The way she'd discover a mugger
In a doorway two blocks ahead.
Let her weigh the bulk of mountains
In both hands and hear dwarf pines
Creak in the wind as crows racket
And phoebes rasp their surnames.
Surely then she'll come home to read
My book and lie beside me
On rumpled sheets, *The Book of Mountains*
Flopping from her hand, the pages
Torn loose and fluttering like moths.

We'll lie there as glad-handed dawn
Strokes our bodies till they clench.
Then later, on a northern slope,
Aroused amid blueberry glades,
We'll riot like renegade priests
Who had forgotten their faith in sin
And made love from the same dry bodies
That for years they've mistaken for mud.
Smug in lecherous April sun,
We'll lie there staring down the sky
While the heat we've made rises
To thrill the sparrows into song
And warm the soil for bluets,
Cinquefoil, starflower, anemone.

When we're safely back in Boston,
The air conditioner will ease us
With flattering groans and wails
While we dream that at the window

A sheath of pines invites us to leap
Into the boughs and drop four stories
To the quilted needles below.
We would enter with conviction
A papery storm-shrouded landscape
Where we'd lick the evergreen scent
From each other's cooling face.

But none of this will happen.
No hike in sultry weather, no
Reading of my mountain saga
Will appease her corporate selfhood.
I might as well burn this book unread.
Far too candid to lie, it recounts
How Manhattan self-consumed
While the mountains sulked in haze,
How she swept my feverish letters
From her desk and crumpled them
Not in blasphemy but rage we share
Against the badly mapped terrain.

www.ingramcontent.com/pod-product-compliance
Lightning Source LLC
LaVergne TN
LVHW090045180726
843489LV00002B/518